In 1859 a hurricane devastat̶e̶d̶ the British Isles, driving a steam clipper laden with passengers, and its cargo of Australian wool, hides and gold, onto the rocks of Anglesey.

The disaster was investigated by Charles Dickens, one of the world's most popular authors, who visited the site of the wreck. The incident led to new shipping forecasts and storm warnings, and improved safety at sea. The wreck of the *Royal Charter* still fascinates us today.

A sailing bill of the *Royal Charter*, outward bound in October 1856 from the Mersey to Melbourne in Australia.

The *Royal Charter*'s record breaking passage halved the time taken by many ships only a few years earlier. In 1850, for example, emigrants leaving Menai Bridge on board the *Infanta*—one of the slate-exporting vessels operated by the Davies family of Treborth, near Bangor—had a 123-day journey ahead of them before Melbourne's Port Philip was sighted.

Charles Dickens (1812-70) is remembered for his great novels, in which he portrayed every level of the society of his day with tenderness, humour and a keen sense of social injustice. Victorian sentimentality was always balanced by an acute eye for detail, his powers of observation honed by years spent as a legal reporter and as a political journalist.

A symbol of Dickens's growing success as an author was his purchase in 1856 of a property in Kent, which he had dreamed of owning since his childhood. However the author's first years at Gad's Hill Place were far from peaceful. In 1857 he began an affair with the actress Ellen Ternan, and as a result his marriage with Catherine (Hogarth) broke up in 1858, amidst private acrimony, rumours and public scandal. However Dickens regained public affection by taking on more theatrical readings of his work, which proved hugely popular and lucrative on both sides of the Atlantic. One of his best received performances proved to be the dramatic storm and shipwreck scene from his 1850 novel *David Copperfield*— reprinted here on page 20.

In April 1859, despite his personal worries, Dickens serialised his novel about the French Revolution, *A Tale of Two Cities*. It appeared in his new weekly journal, called *All the Year Round*. This was incorporated with an earlier periodical, *Household Words*, and became an immediate success with a circulation of more than 100,000. Dickens's new journal also published topical features on matters such as foreign affairs, education, science and technology. At the end of 1859 a much reported news story began to fascinate Charles Dickens, and on 29th December he followed it up with a visit of a few days to the little village of Moelfre, on the east coast of the Isle of Anglesey.

The event that led the great author to this corner of North Wales was the wreck of a ship called the *Royal Charter* in the early hours of 26th October. Dickens would have been fascinated by the reports he read because of their similarities with his own narrative of a terrible shipwreck, but he also wanted to find out about the impact of this disaster on the local community and on those whose loved ones had been lost at sea. His visit was prompted by more than just a reporter's instinct for a good story, for amongst the victims of the wreck were some close relatives of his wife—Peter Hogarth with his wife Georgiana and their young son, together with Peter's elder brother, Robert.

'The Magnificent Steam Clipper'

The *Royal Charter* was an iron-hulled clipper, initially registered at 2,719 imperial tons (2,676 tonnes), though later increased when strengthened, with an overall length of 336 feet (102m). The three-masted ship carried a full complement of sail. She also had a single funnel, for this was a hybrid vessel with auxiliary screws driven by a 200 horse power coal-fired steam engine. Whilst under construction the ship had been sold by Charles Moore & Co to another Liverpool shipping company, Gibbs, Bright & Co, owner of the famous *Great Britain*.

The *Royal Charter* had been launched in 1855 at Sandycroft on the River Dee, in Flintshire. She was a sleek, fast ship, designed with seven watertight and fireproof compartments for safety. She was a luxurious vessel, too, with 28 'state rooms' and a saloon to accommodate 50 first-class passengers as well as second- and third-class and steerage. After some teething troubles, and enduring some fierce storms, the clipper at last proved her mettle with a run of just under 60 days from Plymouth to Melbourne, Australia.

Liverpool bound

On 26th August 1859 the *Royal Charter*, with her reputation as a record-breaking ship secure, sailed out of Hobson's Bay, Melbourne, bound for Liverpool with a crew of 103 (many of them seamen from North Wales or Liverpool). At that point of the voyage, there were 324 passengers, rich and poor, men, women and children. The ship's cargo was made up of copper, hides, wool and gold worth £322,440. The 1850s were the years of the Australian gold rush, and—like the brothers Robert and Peter Hogarth—some passengers were prospectors and miners who carried on their person the gold that had made them rich. The ship's captain was Thomas Taylor, a tough, practical and experienced mariner. The *Royal Charter* rounded the icy waters of Cape Horn and entered the open Atlantic, eventually sighting southern Ireland on 24th October. After putting some passengers ashore at Queenstown (Cobh, in Cork Harbour), the clipper headed up the St George's Channel for the Irish Sea. As the vessel left the coast of Caernarfonshire for Anglesey on 25th October, the southeasterly wind began to rise and the sky darkened over the mountains of Snowdonia. The captain decided to reduce sail and steam on for Liverpool.

The rocks of Moelfre

However, rounding Point Lynas on the northeast corner of Anglesey, the ship was struck by a force 10 storm from east-north-east. The crew signalled by rockets to the pilots at Point Lynas, but no boat could put out in the deteriorating weather. Pushed around towards Moelfre, the clipper was battered by fierce waves and tugged by a swelling tide, and her helmsman began to lose control.

A force 12 hurricane now caught hold of the doomed *Royal Charter*, with howling winds spiralling in from the northeast. The clipper dropped her port anchor at 11pm, and followed with the starboard anchor. Distress guns were fired, but went unheard in the raging tempest. At 1.30am on 26th October the port anchor cable snapped, as did the starboard cable at 2am. The hull soon ran aground, seemingly on sand, but was eventually driven onwards to be trapped by treacherous rock ledges and boulders. Massive waves crashed over the deck. The desperate order was given to cut down the mainmast, and later the foremast. The terror-struck passengers wept and prayed for their lives.

As daylight broke, two men from Moelfre, Thomas Hughes and Mesach Williams, were horrified to see the wrecked ship amidst the crashing waves and flying foam. One ran to the village to get help while the other scrambled down the cliff to the shore. No lifeboat could survive in this hell. A Maltese able seaman aboard the *Royal Charter*, Guze Ruggier (known also as Joseph Rogers), volunteered to try to swim ashore from the ship with a rope tied around his waist. Washed on and off the rocks three times, he finally managed to land the lifeline and eventually a 'bosun's chair' was rigged up from the ship's bow to the shore. The Royal National Life Boat Institution recognised Ruggier's bravery by awarding him their Gold Medal.

The *Great Eastern* survives the Royal Charter Storm in Holyhead Harbour

Isambard Kingdom Brunel's SS Great Eastern, launched in 1858, took refuge from the storm off Holyhead. The breakwater was only partially built, and afforded scant shelter.

R M Ballantyne (1825-1894), the Scottish author of *The Coral Island*, included a vivid description of the hurricane's force in *Man on the Ocean* (1863). Ballantyne too was related to the four drowned members of the Hogarth family—the cousins of Dickens's wife—and as members of the same generation all would have been familiar with one another.

"**A**MONG other tests to which the *Great Eastern* was subjected was the terrible storm of the 25th and 26th October of that year, 1859, in which the *Royal Charter* went down. She lay at anchor in the harbour of Holyhead during that storm. So fierce was the gale that a large part of the breakwater was destroyed, and several vessels went down inside the harbour, while some were driven on shore. For one hour the big ship was as near destruction as she is ever likely to be. Her salvation, under God, was due to the experience and energy of Captain Harrison and his officers. During the whole gale the captain was on the watch, sounding the lead to see if she dragged, and keeping the steam up to be in readiness to put to sea at a moment's notice. The gale roared and whistled through the rigging with indescribable fury. The captain, in trying to pass along the deck, was thrown down, and his waterproof coat was blown to ribbons. The cabin skylights were thrown open with a fearful crash, the glass broken, and deluges of rain and spray poured into the saloons. Two anchors were down, one seven tons, the other three, with eighty and sixty fathoms of chain respectively; but the ground was known to be bad, and the lee-shore rocky, while the waves came curling and writhing into harbour, straining the cables to the utmost, and dashing against the rocks like avalanches of snow. The dash of these billows on the breakwater was like the roar of artillery. All this time the red light at the end of the breakwater shone out cheerily in the midst of a turmoil of spray. At last masses of the timber-work and solid masonry gave way. The gale rose to its fiercest, and one huge billow came rolling in; it towered high above the breakwater; it fell, and the red light was seen no more. The danger was now imminent. The cables could evidently bear no more and the gale was increasing; so the screw was set going, but the wreck of timber from the breakwater fouled it and brought it to a dead-lock. Then the wind veered round more to the north-east, sending a tremendous swell into the harbour, and the Great Eastern began to roll heavily. In this

extremity the paddle engines were set going, and the ship was brought up to her anchors, one of which was raised for the purpose of being dropped in a better position. At this moment the cable of the other anchor parted, and the great ship drifted swiftly toward what seemed certain destruction; but the heavy anchor was let go, and the engines turned on full speed. She swung round head to wind, and was brought up. This was the turning-point. The gale slowly abated, and the *Great Eastern* was saved, while all round her the shores and harbour were strewn with wrecks."

Reports of the time suggest that as many as 36 men from Moelfre and Dulas risked their lives by wading into the crashing waves to help a lucky few survivors on to dry land. Two Irish stable boys employed by the village postmaster also assisted. However, around 7am the *Royal Charter* parted amidships, breaking her back. The bow was separated from the stern and the mizzenmast was felled. By 8am the whole ship was beneath the waves. While many drowned, others were crushed by the collapse of the ship, or pounded to death and mutilated on the rocks. The pocket watches found on the bodies had stopped between 7 and 7.30am. All the women and children died. Only 18 passengers survived, 18 crew members, and 5 riggers, part of a group which had been taken on board the previous day off Bardsey island. As most of the 459 dead were washed ashore in the following days and weeks, they were taken by horse and cart to the local churchyards for burial: 140 were buried at Llanallgo, 64 at Llaneugrad, 45 at Llanfihangel Penrhos Lligwy, and many others in the surrounding parishes.

Reports of disaster

The hurricane raged for another day before subsiding. The storm of the century had sunk 133 ships around the British Isles. The ports, piers and railways of North Wales were devastated, indeed the whole of Britain had taken a battering. However one disaster stood out as the most horrific tragedy of all, and the whole event became known as the 'Royal Charter Storm'.

The story of the ship, its tragic losses and its cargo of gold appeared in every newspaper and periodical. Gold washed up on the shore with the victims certainly enriched a good few villagers and visitors, but soon the law was being enforced by coastguard and militia, and the gold was being accounted for. Of the main cargo, some could be salvaged but much was lost to the waves. As might happen today, parts of the press ran lurid stories of villagers profiteering by pocketing the gold of the victims. The *Daily Telegraph* demanded that they should be given the death penalty, causing great local offence. Charles Dickens decided to investigate, in the last days of December.

Charles Dickens in Anglesey

The island through which Dickens travelled by carriage from Bangor's railway station was a largely poor, rural area, but it was hardly a remote part of the British Isles. Since 1826, Thomas Telford's pioneering Menai Suspension Bridge had routed the A5 to the rapidly growing port of Holyhead, where the great breakwater was still under construction (although part had been breached in the *Royal Charter* storm—see R M Ballantyne's account, opposite). Since 1850, the main rail link to Ireland also crossed the Menai Strait, via Robert Stephenson's Britannia Bridge. The major copper mining enterprise of Parys Mountain, in northeast Anglesey, was now in decline, but its little port at Amlwch was already building ocean-going ships. The inhabitants of a small village such as Moelfre lived by farming, herring fishing or quarrying limestone. The community was mostly Welsh-speaking.

Charles Dickens visited the large rectory in Llanallgo, just to the southwest of Moelfre. The small church of Saint Gallgo had been founded in the sixth century and mostly dated from the fifteenth century. It served as a mortuary after the wreck of the *Royal Charter*. Dickens's host was the Reverend Stephen Roose Hughes, Rector of Llaneugrad & Llanallgo, who together with his wife, Jane Anne, and sisters-in-law (Mary and Margaret Moulsdale), had assisted survivors, organised the identification and burial of the victims and comforted the grieving relatives who made their way to Moelfre. By the time of Dickens's visit, the Rector had written more than a thousand letters of sympathy. The strain affected his health and he would die, aged 47, in 1862. His younger brother Hugh Robert Hughes (1825-1873), curate of Llanfihangel Penrhos Lligwy, had also played a leading part in operations.

The Uncommercial Traveller

When Charles Dickens put pen to paper, he contrasted the calm, orderly scene he witnessed on his arrival in Moelfre with the fury and horror of the terrible storm. He described the recovery of the bodies and their burial, and the admirable work of the rector. Dickens featured some of the moving letters written by the bereaved and also described details such as a gold digger's boots, the sailors' tattoos, or receipts for parrots purchased in Australia. Dickens's account was duly published as 'The Shipwreck' in issue 11 of *All the Year Round*, on 28th January 1860. It was collected together with other essays in a book, *The Uncommercial Traveller*, first published in 1861 and later expanded with the addition of further essays. In the book's introduction, Dickens, writing in the character of an 'uncommercial' traveller, explains his 'general line of business' as travelling *"for the great house of Human Interest Brothers"*— a man inspired by an interest in others, not gain for self.

The Illustrated London News
Saturday 5th November, 1859

THE WRECK OF THE *ROYAL CHARTER*

This vessel was wrecked, as recorded in our Journal last week, on the north-east coast of Anglesea, during the morning of Wednesday, the 26th ult. She was driven upon a shelving ledge of limestone rock (Porth Ynys), distant about five miles from Point Lynas lighthouse, and within a mile from the Moelfre lighthouse.

The *Royal Charter* was built about four years ago; she was of 2719 tons register and 200-horse power. Her owners were Messrs. Gibb, Bright, & Co., of Liverpool. She was an iron vessel, worked by a screw. Appended is a more complete account than we were able to give last week of the terrible disaster. The *Royal Charter* sailed from Melbourne on the 26th of August last, having on board 388 passengers, and a crew, including officers, of 112 persons. She accomplished her passage in two months. On the morning of Monday week she passed Queenstown [the Irish port of Cobh, Cork] and thirteen of the passengers landed in a pilot-boat. The next day the *Royal Charter* took on board from a steam-tug eleven riggers who had been assisting in working a ship to Cardiff. Thus, at the time of the calamity, there were on board 498 persons, and of these only thirty-nine were saved. The ship, as we are informed, had on board but a small cargo, mainly of wool and skins. A more important item of her freight was gold and specie, which at the low-est estimate is put at £500,000. On Tuesday evening there was blowing from the E.N.E, a violent gale, which fell with full force on the ill-fated ship. She arrived off Point Lynas at six o'clock in the evening of Tuesday, and for several hours Captain Taylor continued throwing up signal-rockets, in the hope of attracting the attention of a pilot. None made his appearance. The gale increased in violence; the ship was making leeway, and drifting gradually towards the beach. It was pitch dark; no help was at hand. The captain let go both anchors, but the gale had now increased to a hurricane, and had lashed the sea up to madness. The chains parted; and, notwithstanding that the engines were worked at their full power, the *Royal Charter* continued to drift towards the shore. At three a.m. she struck the rocks in four fathoms of water. The masts and rigging were cut adrift, but this gave no relief. The ship continued to grind and dash upon the rocks. The screw became foul with the drift spars and rigging, and ceased to act. The consequence was that the ship was thrown broadside on to the rocks, and now the terror began. The officers of the ship either hoped against hope, or endeavoured to alleviate the agony of the passengers by assuring them there was no immediate danger.

A Portuguese sailor, Joseph Rogers, conveyed a rope on shore through the heavy surf. Had time been given no doubt every person on board could now have been safely conveyed on shore; but one tremendous wave came after another, playing with the *Royal Charter* like a toy, and swinging her about on the rocks. She divided amidships, and well-nigh all on board were swept into the furious sea.

A few minutes afterwards she also parted at the fore-hatch, and then there was an end. Those who were not killed by the sea were killed by the breaking up of the ship. In the course of a very few moments the work was done, and four hundred and fifty-nine persons were numbered among the dead. It was said by those who visited the scene of the calamity that never was destruction more complete. The ironwork of the vessel was in mere shreds; the woodwork was in chips. The coast and the fields above the cliffs were strewn with fragments of the cargo and of the bedding and clothing. Worse still, the rocks were covered with corpses of men and women frightfully mutilated, and strewn with the sovereigns which the poor creatures had gone so far to seek, and which were now torn from them in so pitiful a way.

The following is the narrative of one of the rescued passengers: "On Tuesday night, when the gale became so strong, opposite the Skerries, the ladies and many of the passengers became exceedingly nervous. For my part, however, I had such confidence in the captain, officers, and ship, that I went to bed at ten o'clock. I could only doze, and was aroused in an hour or two by the fearful storm. I heard a voice in the cabin crying out, 'Come directly, we are all lost; I will take your child; come along directly!' The voice was that of Captain Withers, a passenger, who had lost his own vessel in the South Pacific. I jumped out of bed, and opened his cabin door, but all were gone from there. Hastily putting on a few articles, I ran upon deck. The ship bumped heavily two or three times against the ground. On going into the general saloon I found it crowded with ladies and gentlemen in the utmost state of tremor. Families were all clinging to each other, the young children were crying out piteously, whilst parents were endeavouring to soothe them with cheering hopes. The Reverend Mr Hodge, a Church of England clergyman, belonging to East Retford, instituted a prayer meeting, and a great number of passengers fervently participated in the service. The ship struck, however, so fearfully, and the huge waves came down upon her with such tremendous force, rushing into the cabins through the skylights, broken by the falling rigging and hatches, that all became absorbed in the idea of personal danger. All tried to soothe the ladies and children. Captain Withers came into the cabin, remarking, 'Now, ladies, you need not be at all afraid; we are on a sandy beach, and imbedded in the sand; we are not ten paces from the shore, and the tide will leave us dry; and in ten minutes you will all be safe.' Dr Hatch, a Government medical officer, also cheered the passengers. [*The gravestone of Dr Hatch is shown on page 14.*]

"Captain Taylor came down afterwards to give encouragement, and he made a similar representation, which had the effect of greatly allaying the excitement. Great order was consequently kept on board. At half-past five o'clock the bumping went on worse than ever, until at last the water came rushing in. When daylight began to peep I was knocked by the force of the waves with great violence against the side of the saloon, and the screams were now dreadful. It was impossible to know what to do. I went on deck, but with the greatest difficulty maintained my equilibrium. At this time a great sea came against the broadside, and divided the ship into two, just at the engine-house, as one would smash a pipe-stump, and the sea washed quite through her. The two parts 'slewed' round, and became total wrecks. Parties were carried down with the debris, and as many must have been killed as drowned.

"Having made up my mind that I had best jump overboard on the lee side, I attempted to descend by a rope, but fell deep into the water, which was so thickly strewn with portions of the wreck that I had to open up a passage with my head. I was repeatedly thrown ashore, and as often washed back, until some people on shore managed to rescue me. By this time I was almost worn out and insensible."

The Times
Thursday 27th October, 1859

THE GALE.

LOSS OF THE ROYAL CHARTER.

(BY ELECTRIC AND INTERNATIONAL TELEGRAPH.)

LIVERPOOL, OCT. 27.

A telegram has been received here from Bangor stating that the Royal Charter, from Melbourne, which touched at Queenstown on Monday on her way to Liverpool, has been wrecked in Red-wharf Bay, and that many lives have been lost. She would have a large amount of specie on board, but the quantity is not yet known, as she brings late advices.

Red Wharf Bay is situated about three miles to the westward of Puffin Island, Menai Straits, and six or seven miles to the north-west of Beaumaris. With the exception of the bay, which is very sandy and shallow, the coast is rocky and bold.

The place where the vessel is understood to have been wrecked is not unfavourable for diving operations in calm weather.

The Liverpool pilot-boat No. 12 is reported to have been lost, with all hands.

Some portions of the rails along the Menai Straits are reported to have been washed away, and some of the telegraph wires have been blown down.

"The tug-steamer lying a little off the shore, the lighter lying still nearer to the shore, the boat alongside the lighter, the regularly-turning windlass aboard the lighter, the methodical figures at work, all slowly and regularly heaving up and down with the breathing of the sea, all seemed as much a part of the nature of the place as the tide itself." CHARLES DICKENS

'The Royal Charter at Low Water' by Joseph Josiah Dodd, painted, perhaps from photographs, in 1872.
Reproduced by courtesy of Sotheby's, Chester

William Powell Frith's portrait of 'Charles Dickens in his Study' (at Tavistock House, London) was painted in the year of the shipwreck, 1859.

The Shipwreck *by Charles Dickens*

NEVER HAD I SEEN a year going out, or going on, under quieter circumstances. Eighteen hundred and fifty nine had but another day to live, and truly its end was peace on that seashore that morning.

So settled and orderly was everything seaward, in the bright light of the sun and under the transparent shadows of the clouds, that it was hard to imagine the bay otherwise, for years past or to come, than it was that very day. The tug-steamer lying a little off the shore, the lighter lying still nearer to the shore, the boat alongside the lighter, the regularly-turning windlass aboard the lighter, the methodical figures at work, all slowly and regularly heaving up and down with the breathing of the sea, all seemed as much a part of the nature of the place as the tide itself. The tide was on the flow, and had been for some two hours and a half; there was a slight obstruction in the sea within a few yards of my feet: as if the stump of a tree, with earth enough about it to keep it from lying horizontally on the water, had slipped a little from the land—and as I stood upon the beach and observed it dimpling the light swell that was coming in, I cast a stone over it.

So orderly, so quiet, so regular—the rising and falling of the tug-steamer, the lighter, and the boat—the turning of the windlass—the coming in of the tide—that I myself seemed, to my own thinking, anything but new to the spot. Yet I had never seen it in my life a minute before, and had traversed two hundred miles to get at it. That very morning I had come bowling down, and struggling up, hill-country roads; looking back at snowy summits; meeting courteous peasants, well to do, driving fat pigs and cattle to market; noting the neat and thrifty dwellings, with their unusual quantity of clean white linen drying on the bushes; having windy weather suggested by every cottar's little rick, with its thatched straw-ridged and extra straw-ridged into overlapping compartments like the back of a rhinoceros. Had I not given a lift of fourteen miles to the coast-guardsman (kit and all), who was coming to his spell of duty there, and had we not just now parted company? So it was; but the journey seemed to glide down into the placid sea, with

other chafe and trouble, and for the moment nothing was so calmly and monotonously real under the sunlight as the gentle rising and falling of the water with its freight, the regular turning of the windlass aboard the lighter, and the slight obstruction so very near my feet.

O reader, haply turning this page by the fireside at home, and hearing the night wind rumble in the chimney, that slight obstruction was the uppermost fragment of the wreck of the *Royal Charter*, Australian trader and passenger ship, homeward bound, that struck here on the terrible morning of the twenty-sixth of this October, broke into three parts, went down with her treasure of at least five hundred human lives, and has never stirred since!

From which point, or from which, she drove ashore, stern foremost; on which side, or on which, she passed the little island in the bay, for ages henceforth to be aground certain yards outside her; these are rendered bootless questions by the darkness of that night and the darkness of death. Here she went down.

Even as I stood on the beach, with the words 'Here she went down!' in my ears, a diver in his grotesque dress, dipped heavily over the side of the boat alongside the lighter, and dropped to the bottom. On the shore by the water's edge was a rough tent, made of fragments of wreck, where other divers and workmen sheltered themselves, and where they had kept Christmas day with rum and roast beef, to the destruction of their frail chimney. Cast up among the stones and boulders of the beach were great spars of the long vessel, and masses of iron twisted by the fury of the sea into the strangest forms. The timber was already bleached and iron rusted, and even these objects did no violence to the prevailing air the whole scene wore, of having been exactly the same for years and years.

Yet only two short months had gone since a man, living on the nearest hill-top overlooking the sea, being blown out of bed at about daybreak by the wind that had begun to strip his roof off, and getting upon a ladder with his nearest neighbour to construct some temporary device for keeping his house over his head, saw from the ladder's elevation as he looked down by chance towards the shore, some dark troubled object close in with the land. And he and the other, descending to the beach, and finding the sea mercilessly beating over a great broken ship, had clambered up the stony ways, like staircases without stairs, on which the wild village hangs in little clusters, as fruit hangs on boughs, and had given the alarm. And so, over the hill-slopes, and past the waterfall, and down the gullies where the land drains off into the ocean, the scattered quarrymen and fishermen inhabiting that part of Wales had come running to the dismal sight—their clergymen among them. And as they stood in the leaden morning, stricken with pity, leaning hard against the wind, their breath and vision often failing as the sleet and spray rushed at them from the ever forming and dissolving mountains of sea, and as the wool which was a part of the vessel's cargo blew in with the salt foam and remained upon the land when the foam melted, they saw the ship's life-boat put off from one of the heaps of wreck; and first there were three men in her, and in a moment she capsized, and there were but two; and again she was struck by a vast mass of water, and there was but one; and again she was thrown bottom upward, and that one, with his arm struck through the broken planks and waving as if for the help that could never reach him, went down into the deep.

It was the clergyman himself from whom I heard this, while I stood on the shore, looking in his kind wholesome face as it turned to the spot where the boat had been. The divers were down then, and busy. They were 'lifting' today the gold found yesterday—some five-and-twenty thousand pounds. Of three hundred and fifty thousand pounds' worth of gold, three hundred thousand pounds' worth, in round numbers, was at that time recovered. The great bulk of the remainder was surely and steadily coming up. Some loss of sovereigns there would be, of course; indeed, at first sovereigns had drifted in with the sand, and been scattered far and wide over the beach, like sea-shells; but most other golden treasure would be found. As it was brought up it went aboard the tug-steamer, where good account was taken of it. So tremendous had the force of the sea been when it broke the ship that it had beaten one great ingot of gold deep into a strong and heavy piece of her solid iron-work: in which, also, several loose sovereigns that the

Llanallgo Rectory, and the Parish Church
J M Gahey's lithograph, after a painting by H M Ball
(Reproduced by courtesy of the Parish Authorities of Llaneugrad with Llanallgo)

ingot had swept in before it had been found, as firmly embedded as though the iron had been liquid when they were forced there. It had been remarked of such bodies come ashore, too, as had been seen by scientific men, that they had been stunned to death, and not suffocated. Observation, both of the internal change that had been wrought in them and of their exernal expression, showed death to have been thus merciful and easy. The report was brought, while I was holding such discourse on the beach, that no more bodies had come ashore since last night. It began to be very doubtful whether many more would be thrown up until the north-east winds of the early spring set in. Moreover, a great number of the passengers, and particularly the second-class women passengers, were known to have been in the middle of the ship when she parted, and thus the collapsing wreck would have fallen upon them after yawning open, and would keep them down. A diver made known, even then, that he had come upon the body of a man, and had sought to release it from a great superincumbent weight; but that, finding he could not do so without mutilating the remains, he had left it where it was.

It was the kind and wholesome face I have made mention of as being then beside me that I had purposed to myself to see when I left home for Wales. I had heard of that clergyman as having buried many scores of the

shipwrecked people; of his having opened his house and heart to their agonised friends; of his having used a most sweet and patient diligence for weeks and weeks, in the performance of the forlornest offices that man can render to his kind; of his having most tenderly and thoroughly devoted himself to the dead, and to those who were sorrowing for the dead. I had said to myself, 'In the Christmas season of the year I should like to see that man !' And he had swung the gate of his little garden in coming out to meet me, not half an hour ago.

So cheerful of spirit and guiltless of affectation, as true practical Christianity ever is ! I read more of the New Testament in the fresh frank face going up the village beside me, in five minutes, than I have read in anathematising discourses (albeit put to press with enormous flourishing of trumpets) in all my life. I heard more of the Sacred Book in the cordial voice that had nothing to say about its owner than in all the would-be celestial pairs of bellows that have ever blown conceit at me.

We climbed towards the little church at a cheery pace, among the loose stones, the deep mud, the wet coarse grass, the outlying water, and other obstructions from which frost and snow had lately thawed. It was a mistake (my friend was glad to tell me, on the way) to suppose that the peasantry had shown any superstitious avoidance of the drowned; on the whole, they had done very well, and had assisted readily. Ten shillings had been paid for the bringing of each body up to the church, but the way was steep, and a horse and cart (in which it was wrapped in a sheet) were necessary, and three or four men, and, all things considered, it was not a great price. The people were none the richer for the wreck, for it was the season of the herring shoal—and who could cast nets for fish, and find dead men and women in the draught?

He had the church keys in his hand, and opened the churchyard gate, and opened the church door; and we went in. It is a little church of great antiquity; there is reason to believe that some church has occupied the spot these thousand years or more. The pulpit was gone, and other things usually belonging to the church were gone, owing to its living congregation having deserted it for the neighbouring schoolroom, and yielded it up to the dead. The very Commandments had been shouldered out of their places in the bringing in of the dead; the black wooden tables on which they were painted were askew, and on the stone pavement below them, and on the stone pavement all over the church, were the marks and stains where the drowned had been laid down. The eye, with little or no aid from the imagination, could yet see how the bodies had been turned, and where the head had been and where the feet.

Some faded traces of the wreck of the Australian ship

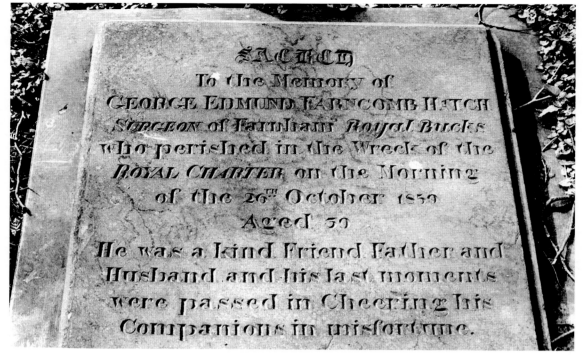

may be discernible on the stone pavement of this little church hundreds of years hence, when the digging for gold in Australia shall have long and long ceased out of the land.

Forty-four shipwrecked men and women lay here at one time, awaiting burial. Here, with weeping and wailing in every room of his house, my companion worked alone for hours, solemnly surrounded by eyes that could not see him, and by lips that could not speak to him, patiently examining the tattered clothing, cutting off buttons, hair, marks from linen, anything that might lead to subsequent identification, studying faces, looking for a scar, a bent finger, a crooked toe, comparing letters sent to him with the ruin about him. 'My dearest brother had bright grey eyes and a pleasant smile', one sister wrote. O poor sister! well for you to be far from here, and keep that as your last remembrance of him!

The ladies of the clergyman's family, his wife and two sisters-in-law, came in among the bodies often. It grew to be the business of their lives to do so. Any new arrival of a bereaved woman would stimulate their pity to compare the description brought with the dread realities. Sometimes they would go back able to say, 'I have found him', or, 'I think she lies there.' Perhaps the mourner, unable to bear the sight of all that lay in the church, would be led in blindfold. Conducted to the spot with many compassionate words, and encouraged to look, she would say, with a piercing cry, 'This is my boy!' and drop insensible on the insensible figure.

He soon observed that in some cases of women, the identification of persons, though complete, was quite at variance with the marks upon the linen; this led him to notice that even the marks upon the linen were sometimes inconsistent with one another; and thus he came to understand that they had dressed in great haste and agitation, and that their clothes had become mixed together. The identification of men by their dress was rendered extremely difficult in consequence of a large proportion of them being dressed alike—in clothes of one kind, that is to say, supplied by shopsellers and outfitters, and not made by single garments but by hundreds. Many of the men were bringing over parrots, and had receipts upon them for the price of the birds; others had bills of exchange in their pockets, or in belts. Some of these documents, carefully unwrinkled and dried, were little less fresh in appearance that day than the present page will be under ordinary circumstances, after having been opened three or four times.

In that lonely place it had not been easy to obtain even such common commodities in towns as ordinary disinfectants. Pitch had been burnt in the church, as the readiest thing at hand, and the frying-pan in which it had bubbled over a brazier of coals was still there, with its ashes. Hard by the communion-table were some boots that had been taken off the drowned and preserved—a gold digger's boot, cut down the leg for its removal—a trodden-down man's ankle-boot with a buff cloth top—and others—soaked and sandy, weedy and salt.

From the church we passed out into the churchyard. Here there lay, at that time, one hundred and forty-five bodies that had come ashore from the wreck. He had buried them, when not identified, in graves containing four each. He had numbered each body in a register describing it, and had placed a corresponding number on each coffin, and over each grave. Identified bodies he had buried singly, in private graves, in another part of the churchyard. Several bodies had been exhumed from the graves of four, as relatives had come from a distance and seen his register; and, when recognised, these have been reburied in private graves, so that the mourners might erect separate headstones over the remains. In all such cases he had performed the funeral service a second time, and the ladies of his house had attended. There had been no offence in the poor ashes when they were brought again to the light of day; the beneficent earth had already absorbed it. The drowned were buried in their clothes. To supply the great sudden demand for coffins he had got all the neighbouring people handy at tools to work the livelong day, and Sunday likewise. The coffins were neatly formed—I had seen two, waiting for occupants, under the lee of the ruined walls of a stone hut on the beach, within call of the tent where the Christmas feast was held. Similarly, one of the graves for four was lying open and ready, here, in the churchyard. So much of the scanty space was already devoted to the wrecked people that the villagers had begun to express uneasy doubts whether they themselves could lie in their own ground, with their forefathers and descendants, by-and-by. The churchyard being but a step from the clergyman's dwelling-house, we crossed to the latter; the white surplice was hanging up near the door ready to be put on at any time for a funeral service.

The cheerful earnestness of this good Christian minister was as consolatory as the circumstances out of which it shone were sad. I never have seen anything more delightfully genuine than the calm dismissal by himself and his household of all they had undergone as a simple duty that was quietly done and ended. In speaking of it they spoke with great compassion for the bereaved; but laid no stress upon their own hard share in those weary weeks, except as it had attached many people to them as friends, and elicited many touching expressions of gratitude. This clergyman's brother—himself the clergyman of two adjoining parishes, who had buried thirty-four of the bodies in his own churchyard, and who had done to them all that his brother had done as to the larger number—must be understood as included in the family. He was there with his neatly arranged papers, and made no more account of his trouble than anybody else did. Down to yesterday's post outward, my clergyman alone had written one thousand and seventy-five letters to relatives and friends of the lost people. In the absence of self-assertion it was only through my now and then delicately putting a question as the occasion arose, that I became informed of these things. It was only when I had remarked again and again, in the church, on the awful nature of the scene of death he had been required so closely to familiarise himself with for the soothing of the living, that he had casually said, without the least abatement of his cheerfulness, 'Indeed, it had rendered him unable for a time to eat or drink more than a little coffee now and then, and a piece of bread.'

In this noble modesty, in this beautiful simplicity, in this serene avoidance of the least attempt to 'improve' an occasion which might be supposed to have sunk of its own weight into my heart, I seemed to have happily come, in a few steps, from the churchyard, with its open grave, which was the type of Death, to the Christian dwelling side by side with it, which was the type of Resurrection. I never shall think of the former without the latter. The two will always rest side by side in my memory. If I had lost anyone dear to me in this unfortunate ship, if I had made a voyage from Australia to look at the grave in the churchyard, I should go away thankful to God that that house was so close to it, and that its shadow by day and its domestic lights by night fell upon the earth in which its Master had so tenderly laid my dear one's head.

The references that naturally arose out of our conversation to the descriptions sent down of shipwrecked persons, and to the gratitude of relations and friends, made me very anxious to see some of those letters. I was presently seated before a shipwreck of papers, all bordered with black, and from them I made the following few extracts:

A mother writes:

REVEREND SIR,—Amongst the many who perished on your shore was numbered my beloved son. I was only just recovering from a severe illness, and this fearful affliction has caused a relapse, so that I am unable at present to go to identify the remains of the loved and lost. My darling son would have been sixteen on Christmas-day next. He was a most amiable and obedient child, early taught the way of salvation. We fondly hoped that as a British seaman he might be an ornament to his profession, but, 'it is well'; I feel assured my dear boy is now with the redeemed. Oh, he did not wish to go this last voyage! On the fifteenth of October I received a letter from him from Melbourne, date August twelfth; he wrote in high spirits, and in conclusion he says: 'Pray for a fair breeze, dear mamma, and I'll not forget to whistle for it! and, God permitting, I shall see you and all my little pets again. Good-bye, dear mother—good-bye, dearest parents. Good-bye, dear brother.' Oh, it was indeed an eternal farewell. I do not apologise for thus writing you, for oh, my heart is so very sorrowful.

A husband writes:

MY DEAR KIND SIR,—Will you kindly inform me whether there are any initials upon the ring and guard you have in possession, found, as the Standard says, last Tuesday? Believe me, my dear sir, when I say that I cannot express my deep gratitude in words sufficiently for your kindness to me on that fearful and appalling day. Will you tell me what I can do for you, and will you write me a consoling letter to prevent my mind from going astray?

A widow writes:

Left in such a state as I am, my friends and I thought it best that my dear husband should be buried where he lies, and, much as I should have liked to have had it otherwise, I must submit. I feel, from all I have heard of you, that you will see it done decently and in order. Little does it signify to us, when the soul has departed, where this poor body lies, but we who are left behind would do all we can to show how we loved them. This is denied me, but it is God's hand that afflicts us, and I try to submit. Some day I may be able to visit the spot, and see where he lies, and erect a simple stone to his memory. Oh! it will be long, long before I forget that dreadful night! Is there such a thing in the vicinity, or any shop in Bangor, to which I could send for a small picture of Moelfra or Llanallgo church, a spot now sacred to me?

Another widow writes:

I have received your letter this morning, and do thank you most kindly for the interest you have taken about my dear husband, as well for the sentiments yours contains, evincing the spirit of a Christian who can sympathise with those who, like myself, are broken down with grief. May God bless and sustain you, and all in connection with you, in this great trial. Time may roll on and bear all its sons away, but your name as a disinterested person will stand in history, and, as successive years pass, many a widow will think of your noble conduct, and the tears of gratitude flow down many a cheek, the tribute of a thankful heart, when other things are forgotten for ever.

A father writes:

I am at a loss to find words to sufficiently express my gratitude to you for your kindness to my son Richard upon the melancholy occasion of his visit to his dear brother's body, and also for your ready attention in pronouncing our beautiful burial service over my poor unfortunate son's remains. God grant that your prayers over him may reach the Mercy Seat, and that his soul may be received (through Christ's intercession) into Heaven! His dear mother begs me to convey to you her heartfelt thanks.

Those who were received at the clergyman's house write thus, after leaving it:

DEAR & NEVER-TO-BE FORGOTTEN FRIENDS, —I arrived here yesterday morning without accident, and am about to proceed to my home by railway. I am overpowered when I think of you and your hospitable home. No words could speak language suited to my heart. I refrain. God reward you with the same measure you have meted with!

I enumerate no names, but embrace you all.

MY BELOVED FRIENDS,—This is the first day that I have been able to leave my bedroom since I returned, which will explain the reason of my not writing sooner. If I could only have had my last melancholy hope realised in recovering the body of my beloved and lamented son, I should have returned home somewhat comforted, and I think I could then have been comparatively resigned. I fear now there is but little prospect, and I mourn as one without hope.

The only consolation to my distressed mind is in having been so feelingly allowed by you to leave the matter in your hands, by whom I well know that everything will be done that can be, according to arrangements made before I left the scene of the awful catastrophe, both as to the identification of my dear son, and also his interment.

I feel most anxious to hear whether anything fresh has transpired since I left you; will you add another to the many deep obligations I am under to you by writing to me? And, should the body of my dear and unfortunate son be identified, let me hear from you immediately, and I will come again. Words cannot express the gratitude I feel I owe to you for all your benevolent aid, your kindness, and your sympathy.

MY DEARLY BELOVED FRIENDS,—I arrived in safety at my house yesterday, and a night's rest has restored and tranquillised me. I must again repeat, that language has no words by which I can express my sense of obligation to you. You are enshrined in my heart of hearts.

I have seen him! and can now realise my misfortune more than I have hitherto been able to do. Oh, the bitterness of the cup I drink! But I bow submissive. God must have done right. I do not want to feel less, but to acquiesce more simply.

There were some Jewish passengers on board the *Royal Charter,* and the gratitude of the Jewish people is feelingly expressed in the following letter, bearing date from 'the office of the Chief Rabbi':

REVEREND SIR,—I cannot refrain from expressing to you my heartfelt thanks on behalf of those of my flock whose relatives have unfortunately been among

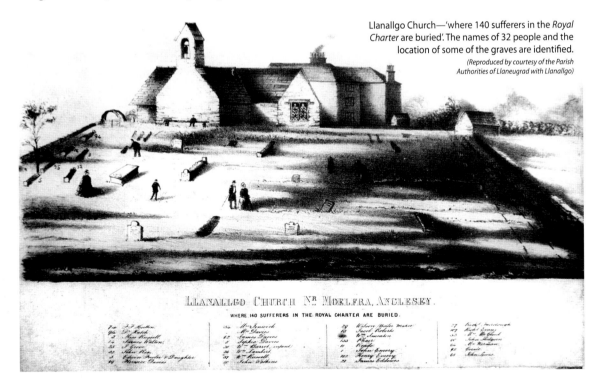

Llanallgo Church—'where 140 sufferers in the *Royal Charter* are buried'. The names of 32 people and the location of some of the graves are identified.
(Reproduced by courtesy of the Parish Authorities of Llaneugrad with Llanallgo)

those who perished at the late wreck of the *Royal Charter*. You have, indeed, like Boaz, 'not left off your kindness to the living and the dead.'

You have not alone acted kindly towards the living by receiving them hospitably at your house, and energetically assisting them in their mournful duty, but also towards the dead, by exerting yourself to have our co-religionists buried in our ground and according to our rites. May our heavenly Father reward you for your acts of humanity and true philanthropy!

The 'Old Hebrew congregation of Liverpool' thus express themselves through their secretary:

REVEREND SIR,—The wardens of this congregation have learned with great pleasure that, in addition to those indefatigable exertions at the scene of the late disaster to the *Royal Charter*, which have received universal recognition, you have very benevolently employed your valuable efforts to assist such members of our faith as have sought the bodies of lost friends to give them burial in our consecrated grounds, with the observances and rites prescribed by the ordinances of our religion. The wardens desire me to take the earliest available opportunity to offer to you, on behalf of our community, the expression of their warm acknowledgements and grateful thanks, and their sincere wishes for your continued welfare & prosperity.

Modern exploration of the wreck began with the dives of the 1970s and continued until recent times. Relics recovered include personal possessions such as jewellery, gold sovereigns and nuggets.

A Jewish gentleman writes:

REVEREND AND DEAR SIR,—I take the opportunity of thanking you right earnestly for the promptness you displayed in answering my note with full particulars concerning my much-lamented brother, and I also herein beg to express my sincere regard for the willingness you displayed and for the facility you afforded for getting the remains of my poor brother exhumed. It has been to us a most sorrowful and painful event, but when we meet with such friends as yourself, it in a measure, somehow or other, abates that mental anguish, and makes the suffering so much easier to be borne. Considering the circumstances connected with my poor brother's fate, it does, indeed, appear a hard one. He had been away in all seven years; he returned four years ago to see his family. He was then engaged to a very amiable young lady. He had been very successful abroad, and was now returning to fulfil his sacred vow; he brought all his property with him in gold, uninsured. We heard from him when the ship stopped at Queenstown, when he was in the highest of hope, and in a few short hours afterwards all was washed away.

Mournful in the deepest degree, but too sacred for quotation here, were the numerous references to those miniatures of women worn round the necks of rough men (and found there after death), those locks of hair, those scraps of letters, those many many slight memorials of hidden tenderness. One man cast up by the sea bore about him, printed on a perforated lace card, the following singular (and unavailing) charm:

A BLESSING. May the blessing of God await thee. May the sun of glory shine around thy bed; and may the gates of plenty, honour, and happiness be ever open to thee. May no sorrow distress thy days; may no grief disturb thy nights. May the pillow of peace kiss thy cheek, and the pleasures of imagination attend thy dreams; and when length of years makes thee tired of earthly joys, and the curtain of death gently closes around thy last sleep of human existence, may the Angel of God attend thy bed, and take care that the expiring lamp of life shall not receive one rude blast to hasten on its extinction.

A sailor had these devices on his right arm: 'Our Saviour on the Cross, the forehead of the crucifix and the vesture stained red; on the lower part of the arm a man and a woman; on one side of the cross, the appearance of a half moon, with a face; on the other side, the sun; on the top of the cross, the letters I.H.S.; on the left arm, a man and woman dancing, with an effort to delineate the female's dress; under which, initials.'

Another seaman 'had, on the lower part of the right arm, the device of a sailor and a female; the man holding the Union Jack with a streamer, the folds of which waved over her head, and the end of it was held in her hand. On the upper part of the arm, a device of Our Lord on the Cross, with stars surrounding the head of the cross, and one large star on the side in Indian ink. On the left arm, a flag, a true lover's knot, a face, and initials.'

This tattooing was found still plain, below the discoloured outer surface of a mutilated arm, when such surface was carefully scraped away with a knife. It is not improbable that the perpetuation of this marking custom among seamen may be referred back to their desire to be identified, if drowned and flung ashore.

It was some time before I could sever myself from the many interesting papers on the table, and then I broke bread and drank wine with the kind family before I left them. As I brought the coast-guard down, so I took the postman back, with his leathern wallet, walking-stick, bugle, and terrier dog. Many a heart-broken letter had he brought to the Rectory House within two months; many a benignantly painstaking answer had he carried back.

As I rode along, I thought of the many people, inhabitants of this mother country, who would make pilgrimages to the little churchyard in the years to come; I thought of the many people in Australia, who would have an interest in such a shipwreck, and would find their way here when they visit the Old World; I thought of the writers of all the wreck of letters I had left upon the table; and I resolved to place this little record where it stands. Convocations, Conferences, Diocesan Epistles, and the like, will do a great deal for religion, I dare say, and Heaven send they may! but I doubt if they will ever do their master's service half so well, in all the time they last, as the Heavens have seen it done in this bleak spot upon the rugged coast of Wales.

Family connections of Stephen Roose Hughes
Dickens's host was born at Madyn Dysw, Amlwch, in 1814.

His father, **William Hughes**, a farmer, having been awarded a lucrative contract to cart the copper ore down from Parys Mountain to Porth Amlwch, developed many other business connections with the Anglesey copper trade, including interests in shipping.

The Revd. Stephen Roose Hughes

Stephen Roose Hughes's maternal grandfather, **Stephen Roose**, was a half-brother (his father had married twice) of **Jonathon Roose** (1731-1813), the Derbyshire mining agent who led the search for Parys Mountain's richest sources of copper ore. Jonathon's gravestone at Saint Eleth's Church, Amlwch, records that in March 1768 … *"He first yon mountain's wondrous riches found,*
First drew its minerals blushing from the ground,
He heard the miners' first exulting shout
Then toil'd near 50 years to guide its treasure out."

Jonathon Roose's fame was assured, but by the time of the shipwreck in 1859 the years of Anglesey's copper-boom were over—brought to an end by ever-increasing competition from mines abroad. Australian copper formed part of the cargo of the ill-fated *Royal Charter*.

Had I lost the friend of my life, in the wreck of the *Royal Charter*; had I lost my betrothed, the more than friend of my life; had I lost my maiden daughter, had I lost my hopeful boy, had I lost my little child; I would kiss the hands that worked so busily and gently in the church, and say, 'None better could have touched the form, though it had lain at home.' I could be sure of it, I could be thankful for it: I could be content to leave the grave near the house the good family pass in and out of every day, undisturbed, in the little churchyard where so many are so strangely brought together.

Without the name of the clergyman to whom—I hope, not without carrying comfort to some heart at some time—I have referred, my reference would be as nothing. He is the Reverend Stephen Roose Hughes, of Llanallgo, near Moelfra, Anglesey. His brother is the Reverend Hugh Robert Hughes, of Penrhos Alligwy.

Charles Dickens, 'The Uncommercial Traveller'—January 1860

An extract from
David Copperfield
(1850)

I PUT UP AT THE OLD INN, and went down to look at the sea; staggering along the street, which was strewn with sand and sea-weed, and with flying blotches of sea-foam; afraid of falling slates and tiles; and holding by people I met, at angry corners. Coming near the beach, I saw, not only the boatmen, but half the people of the town, lurking behind buildings; some, now and then braving the fury of the storm to look away to sea, and blown sheer out of their course in trying to get zigzag back.

Joining these groups, I found bewailing women whose husbands were away in herring or oyster boats, which there was too much reason to think might have foundered before they could run in anywhere for safety. Grizzled old sailors were among the people, shaking their heads, as they looked from water to sky, and muttering to one another; shipowners, excited and uneasy; children, huddling together, and peering into old faces; even stout mariners, disturbed and anxious, levelling their glasses at the sea from behind places of shelter, as if they were surveying an enemy.

The tremendous sea itself, when I could find sufficient pause to look at it, in the agitation of the blinding wind, the flying stones and sand, and the awful noise, confounded me. As the high watery walls came rolling in, and, at their highest, tumbled into surf, they looked as if the least would engulf the town. As the receding wave swept back with a hoarse roar, it seemed to scoop out deep caves in the beach, as if its purpose was to undermine the earth. When some white-headed billows thundered on, and dashed themselves to pieces before they reached the land, every fragment of the late whole seemed possessed by the full might of its wrath, rushing to be gathered to the composition of another monster. Undulating hills were changed to valleys, undulating valleys (with a solitary storm-bird sometimes skimming through them) were lifted up to hills; masses of water shivered and shook the beach with a booming sound; every shape tumultuously rolled on, as soon as made, to change its shape and place, and beat another shape and place away; the ideal shore on the horizon, with its towers and buildings, rose and fell; the clouds flew fast and thick; I seemed to see a rending and up-heaving of all nature …

… There was a dark gloom in my solitary chamber, when I at length returned to it; but I was tired now, and, getting into bed again, fell—off a tower and down a precipice—into the depths of sleep. I have an impression that for a long time, though I dreamed of being else-where and in a variety of scenes, it was always blowing in my dream. At length, I lost that feeble hold upon real-ity, and was engaged with two dear friends, but who they were I don't know, at the siege of some town in a roar of cannonading.

The thunder of the cannon was so loud and incessant, that I could not hear something I much desired to hear, until I made a great exertion and awoke. It was broad day—eight or nine o'clock; the storm raging, in lieu of the batteries; and some one knocking and calling at my door. "What is the matter?" I cried.

"A wreck! Close by!"
I sprang out of bed, and asked, what wreck?

"A schooner, from Spain or Portugal, laden with fruit and wine. Make haste, sir, if you want to see her! It's thought, down on the beach, she'll go to pieces every moment."

The excited voice went clamouring along the stair-case; and I wrapped myself in my clothes as quickly as I could, and ran into the street. Numbers of people were there before me, all running in one direction, to the beach. I ran the same way, outstripping a good many, and soon came facing the wild sea.

The wind might by this time have lulled a little, though not more sensibly than if the cannonading I had dreamed of, had been diminished by the silencing of half-a-dozen guns out of hundreds. But the sea, having upon it the additional agitation of the whole night, was infinitely more terrific than when I had seen it last. Every appearance it had then presented, bore the ex-pression of being swelled; and the height to which the breakers rose, and, looking over one another, bore one another down, and rolled in, in interminable hosts, was most appalling.

In the difficulty of hearing anything but wind and waves, and in the crowd, and the unspeakable confusion, and my first breathless efforts to stand against the weather, I was so confused that I looked out to sea for the wreck, and saw nothing but the foaming heads of the great waves. A half-dressed boatman, standing next me, pointed with his bare arm (a tattoo'd arrow on it, point-ing in the same direction) to the left. Then, O great Heaven, I saw it, close in upon us!

One mast was broken short off, six or eight feet from the deck, and lay over the side, entangled in a maze of sail and rigging; and all that ruin, as the ship rolled and beat—which she did without a moment's pause, and with a violence quite inconceivable—beat the side as if it would stave it in. Some efforts were even then being made to cut this portion of the wreck away; for, as the ship, which was broadside on, turned towards us in her rolling, I plainly descried her people at work with axes, especially one active figure with long curling hair, con-spicuous among the rest. But, a great cry, which was audible even above the wind and water, rose from the shore at this moment; the sea, sweeping over the rolling wreck, made a clean breach, and carried men, spars, casks, planks, bulwarks, heaps of such toys, into the boil-ing surge.

The second mast was yet standing, with the rags of a rent sail, and a wild confusion of broken cordage flapping to and fro. The ship had struck once, the same boatman hoarsely said in my ear, and then lifted in and struck again. I understood him to add that she was parting amidships, and I could readily suppose so, for the rolling and beating were too tremendous for any human work to suffer long. As he spoke, there was another great cry of pity from the beach; four men arose with the wreck out of the deep, clinging to the rigging of the remaining mast; uppermost the active figure with the curling hair.

There was a bell on board; and as the ship rolled and dashed, like a desperate creature driven mad, now show-ing us the whole sweep of her deck, as she turned on her beam-ends towards the shore, now nothing but her keel, as she sprang wildly over and turned towards the sea, the bell rang; and its sound, the knell of those un-happy men, was borne towards us on the wind. Again we lost her, and again she rose. Two men were gone. The agony on shore increased. Men groaned, and clasped their hands; women shrieked, and turned away their faces. Some ran wildly up and down along the beach, crying for help where no help could be. I found myself one of these, frantically imploring a knot of sailors whom I knew, not to let those two lost creatures perish before our eyes.

They were making out to me, in an agitated way—I don't know how, for the little I could hear I was scarcely composed enough to understand—that the life-boat had been bravely manned an hour ago, and could do nothing; and that as no man would be so desperate as to attempt to wade off with a rope, and establish a communication with the shore, there was nothing left to try; when I noticed that some new sensation moved the people on the beach, and saw them part, and Ham come breaking through them to the front.

I ran to him—as well as I know, to repeat my appeal for help. But, distracted though I was, by a sight so new to me and terrible, the determination in his face. and his look, out to sea—exactly the same look as I remembered in connection with the morning after Emily's flight—awoke me to a knowledge of his danger. I held him back with both arms; and implored the men with whom I had been speaking, not to listen to him, not to do murder, not to let him stir from off that sand!

Another cry arose on shore; and looking to the wreck, we saw the cruel sail, with blow on blow, beat off the lower of the two men, and fly up in triumph round the active figure left alone upon the mast. Against such a sight, and against such determination as that of the calmly desperate man who was already accustomed to lead half the people present, I might as hopefully have entreated the wind." Mas'r Davy," he said, cheerily grasping me by both hands, "if my time is come, 'tis come. It 'tan't, I'll bide it. Lord above bless you, and bless all! Mates, make me ready! I'm a going off!"

I was swept away, but not unkindly, to some distance, where the people around me made me stay; urging, as I confusedly perceived, that he was bent on going, with help or without, and that I should endanger the precautions for his safety by troubling those with whom they rested. I don't know what I answered, or what they rejoined; but, I saw hurry on the beach, and men running with ropes from a capstan that was there, and penetrating into a circle of figures that hid him from me. Then, I saw him standing alone, in a seaman's frock and trousers: a rope in his hand, or slung to his wrist: another round his body: and several of the best men holding, at a little distance, to the latter, which he laid out himself, slack upon the shore, at his feet.

The wreck, even to my unpractised eye, was breaking up. I saw that she was parting in the middle, and that the life of the solitary man upon the mast hung by a thread. Still, he clung to it. He had a singular red cap on,—not like a sailor's cap, but of a finer colour; and as the few yielding planks between him and destruction rolled and bulged, and his anticipative death-knell rang, he was seen by all of us to wave it. I saw him do it now, and thought I was going distracted, when his action brought an old remembrance to my mind of a once dear friend.

Ham watched the sea, standing alone, with the silence of suspended breath behind him, and the storm before, until there was a great retiring wave, when, with a backward glance at those who held the rope which was made fast round his body, he dashed in after it, and in a moment was buffeting with the water; rising with the hills, falling with the valleys, lost beneath the foam; then drawn again to land. They hauled in hastily.

He was hurt. I saw blood on his face, from where I stood; but he took no thought of that. He seemed hurriedly to give them some directions for leaving him more free—or so I judged from the motion of his arm—and was gone as before.

And now he made for the wreck, rising with the hills, falling with the valleys, lost beneath the rugged foam, borne in towards the shore, borne on towards the ship, striving hard and valiantly. The distance was nothing, but the power of the sea and wind made the strife deadly. At length he neared the wreck. He was so near, that with one more of his vigorous strokes he would be clinging to it,—when a high, green, vast hill-side of water, moving on shoreward, from beyond the ship, he seemed to leap up into it with a mighty bound, and the ship was gone!

Some eddying fragments I saw in the sea, as if a mere cask had been broken, in running to the spot where they were hauling in. Consternation was in every face. They drew him to my very feet—insensible—dead. He was carried to the nearest house; and, no one preventing me now, I remained near him, busy, while every means of restoration were tried, but he had been beaten to death by the great wave, and his generous heart was stilled for ever.

The Storm's legacy

In 1859 the material cost to the United Kingdom of marine accidents and shipwrecks was over £1.5 million. Damage from the _Royal Charter_ storm had been extensive across western Britain from the Channel coast to Scotland, with the loss of over eight hundred lives on land and at sea. The impact of the storm went far beyond the victims and their relatives.

Mapping the weather

In 1853 FitzRoy became meteorological adviser to the Board of Trade and encouraged the distribution of sturdy barometers for predicting storms. In 1859 he joined the management committee of the Royal National Lifeboat Institution. When the _Royal Charter_ storm took so many lives, FitzRoy studied its meteorology intently, presenting a paper on the subject to the Royal Society.

FitzRoy was determined to set up a system whereby weather reports could be telegraphed from all over Britain (and also six continental sites), and the data converted into a 'synoptic chart' for each area—the weather map with which we are familiar today. This would provide seafarers with priceless, life-saving intelligence about marine conditions. By 1861 storm warnings from his office were being issued and published in the press. FitzRoy also introduced storm signals (cones and cylinders) that could be hoisted at shore stations. In 1862 he published a meteorological treatise called _The Weather Book_.

FitzRoy's achievements were remarkable and internationally recognised, but he was a deeply troubled man, worried about his health and his finances. The year 1859 had brought not only the _Royal Charter_ storm, but an intellectual storm following the publication of Charles Darwin's _Origin of Species_. FitzRoy was a Christian fundamentalist who opposed all notion of evolution, and he bitterly attacked the theories of his erstwhile travelling companion at a famous public debate in Oxford. His weather forecasting methods also came under increasing criticism from rivals and from commercial interests, and any inaccuracies were derided in the press.

Ever more stressed and confused, FitzRoy committed suicide in 1865. Despite this sad end to his life, FitzRoy's work with meteorology and forecasting was, in the longer term, of great benefit to mankind. The lessons of the _Royal Charter_ tragedy had been learned. In 2002 the UK shipping forecast, broadcast daily on the BBC, re-named a sea area (previously known as Finisterre) as FitzRoy, in his honour.

While the novelist Charles Dickens was examining the stories of the ordinary people caught up in the disaster, mariners and scientists were studying the nature of the hurricane and its implications for shipping. One man who believed the tragedy had been avoidable was Rear Admiral Robert FitzRoy (1805-65). FitzRoy was a brilliant navigator and surveyor, who had commanded HMS _Beagle_ while charting the coast of South America. On his second voyage in the _Beagle_ (1831-36), FitzRoy had been accompanied by the young naturalist Charles Darwin (1809-82). Darwin greatly admired FitzRoy, although at times the naval officer could be touchy and difficult. FitzRoy was elected to parliament in 1842, supporting legislation to regulate the Merchant Navy, and from 1843-43 served as Governor of New Zealand, where his fair dealing with the Maoris earned him few friends amongst the British settlers. In 1851 he was elected a member of Britain's most prestigious scientific association, the Royal Society.

Robert FitzRoy

The wreck of the Hindlea
26th October 1959

In 1959, one hundred years and one day after the *Royal Charter Storm*, a hurricane again struck the eastern coast of Anglesey. This time the victim was a 650-ton Cardiff coaster, the *Hindlea*. Thanks to a new generation of tough motor-powered lifeboats, Moelfre coxswain Richard Evans was able to save the crew before the ship crashed into the rocks. He was presented with the Gold Medal of the Royal National Lifeboat Institution, the first of two such awards. The courage of Moelfre's remarkable lifeboat crews over the years remains an enduring memorial to those who perished in 1859.

The horrific fate of the victims of the *Royal Charter* did not fade easily from the public imagination, but as the years passed new technologies such as radio made it safer to travel by sea.

Safety at sea

The captain of the *Royal Charter* had been officially cleared of any negligence which may have contributed to the shipwreck. Nor had there been any technical failures in marine safety procedures. In its final hours the *Royal Charter* had passed several major Anglesey lighthouses, such as South Stack (1809), the Skerries (1716 and 1804) and Point Lynas (1779 and 1835). The functioning of these lights had not played a part in the disaster—although the Assistant Keeper at South Stack, Jack Jones, had been struck by a falling rock during the storm and later died from his injuries. However, the widespread shock that followed the *Royal Charter* disaster prompted a new examination of all aspects of safety at sea.

A Royal Commission was duly set up to investigate the 'Conditions and Management of Lights, Buoys and Beacons'. This was a timely inquiry, for the year 1860 saw the shipwreck of 250 vessels during a single fortnight. The Commission was chaired by Admiral Baillie Hamilton, and had a thorough remit, visiting British and French lighthouses to evaluate quality, location, management and costs. The Commission paid special attention to recent technological advances in lighting and optics. Lighthouse keepers and lifeboatmen were much admired in the Victorian era for their public service and frequent bravery in preventing shipwreck.

William Scoresby's 'Magnetical Research'

William Scoresby (1789–1857), the son of a Yorkshire whaler, began his working life aboard his father's ship. Developing an interest in the sciences, he attended natural philosophy and chemistry classes at Edinburgh University. During subsequent whaling expeditions he made important discoveries in Arctic geography, meteorology and oceanography, and he searched for the Northwest Passage. Whilst he was away in Greenland waters, his wife died. He entered the Church but continued with his scientific work.

Navigators were presented with a problem when iron-hulled vessels began to be built in the 1840s: serious errors were observed in the bearings taken from marine compasses. In 1856 the Reverend Dr Scoresby was granted free passage—from the Mersey to Melbourne and back—on the maiden voyage of the *Royal Charter* (commanded by Captain Francis Boyce), in order to further his studies of terrestrial magnetism. Scoresby's scientific observations appeared posthumously in the *Journal of a Voyage to Australia for Magnetical Research* (1859), in which measures to correct compass deviations are proposed. The *Journal's* fascinating second part, a 'Narrative of the Voyage', is a detailed day-by-day chronicle of life aboard the *Royal Charter*. Weathering gales and a terrible cyclone', she 'behaved splendidly'. The descriptions of the passengers' living conditions are of particular interest.